Painter of Rural America:

WILLIAM SIDNEY MOUNT

1807-1868

by Alfred Frankenstein

Introduction by Jane des Grange

Circulated by the INTERNATIONAL EXHIBITIONS FOUNDATION

WILLIAM SIDNEY MOUNT, 1807-1868

NATIONAL GALLERY OF ART, WASHINGTON, D.C.   *November 23, 1968 — January 5, 1969*
CITY ART MUSEUM OF ST. LOUIS, MISSOURI   *January 18 — February 15, 1969*
WHITNEY MUSEUM OF AMERICAN ART, NEW YORK   *March 3 — April 15, 1969*
M. H. de YOUNG MEMORIAL MUSEUM, SAN FRANCISCO   *May 1-31, 1969*

DESIGNED BY KURT WIENER. PRINTED IN THE
UNITED STATES BY H. K. PRESS, WASHINGTON

I DO NOT APPROVE OF OUR BEST PICTURES BEING OWNED BY MISERS, SO THAT ARTISTS MUST TAKE A NOTE AND A HAT UNDER HIS ARM BEFORE HE CAN HAVE A SIGHT OF SOME FAVORITE PICTURE. THE BEST WORKS SHOULD BE OBTAINED AND PLACED IN SOME PUBLIC GALLERY FOR THE BENIFIT OF AMATEURS AND ARTISTS.

—*WILLIAM SIDNEY MOUNT*

ACKNOWLEDGMENTS

Mr. and Mrs. Ward Melville of Stony Brook, Long Island, are very much aware of the importance of preserving our heritage; they are very much interested in Long Island and its contributions to the rest of the country; they are very much interested in Stony Brook and her people. Therefore it is not strange that in 1943 when they first acquired several Mount paintings they were quite willing to share them with the community. The Melville Collection, housed at the Suffolk Museum in Stony Brook, is now the largest collection of Mount paintings and Mountiana in the country.

Rarely does the "immortal residue" of an artist survive in the quantity that it does in the Suffolk Museum's collections. There are ten diaries, eight journals, nearly two hundred pencil sketches, several hundred letters to and from W. S. Mount, photographs, patent papers and sketch books, relics of Mount's library, and patent models of his concaved-back violin, innumerable dissertations on painting techniques, light, oils and pigments and on his philosophy of work and living.

As sponsors of this exhibition it gives us great pleasure to share our collection; but the scope of the present exhibition would not have been possible without the cooperation of the many farsighted museums that acquired Mount paintings for their collections; most— many years ago. The generous cooperation and interest of the directors of the lending museums and the private collectors is acknowledged and appreciated:

> Mr. & Mrs. J. William Middendorf, II
> Mr. & Mrs. Malcolm E. Smith
> Miss Helen Rommel
> The Berkshire Museum
> The Corcoran Gallery of Art
> The Detroit Institute of Arts
> The Metropolitan Museum of Art
> Museum of Fine Arts, Boston
> National Gallery of Art
> New York State Historical Association
> National Collection of Fine Arts, Smithsonian Institution
> Pennsylvania Academy of the Fine Arts

We wish also to express our indebtedness to the directors of the museums who committed themselves to this exhibition "on faith" in the artist, William Sidney Mount: John Walker, Director, National Gallery of Art; Charles E. Buckley, Director, City Art Museum of St. Louis: Lloyd Goodrich, Director Emeritus, and John I. H. Baur, Director, Whitney Museum of American Art; Jack R. McGregor, Director, M. H. de Young Memorial Museum, San Francisco.

As Director of the Suffolk Museum, I am particularly indebted to Alfred Frankenstein, who has excerpted the catalog notes from his forthcoming book on William Sidney Mount; to William P. Campbell, to William W. Morrison, and Henry Beville of the National Gallery of Art; to Annemarie H. Pope, President, International Exhibitions Foundation; and Kurt Wiener of the H. K. Press for the awareness of our limitations, their continued cooperation and unfailing confidence.

J. d. G.

WILLIAM SIDNEY MOUNT

The lives and works of few American painters are as well documented as are the life and work of William Sidney Mount. As he himself admitted, scribbling was one of his favorite vices — and he was very good at it. He kept voluminous diaries and journals; he preserved many of the letters he received and drafts of many he sent; and although he usually declined to provide journalists and historians with information about himself, he often complied with their requests in secret, sketching autobiographies and squirreling them away. The existing Mount documents run to about four thousand pages, and they are preserved in two large and two small repositories. The two large repositories are the Suffolk Museum at Stony Brook, Long Island, and the New-York Historical Society; between them, these two organizations possess perhaps three of the four thousand pages. The small repositories are the Public Library at Smithtown, Long Island, near Stony Brook, which has two diaries and some letters, and the

SELF-PORTRAIT 1832

collection of Theodore Stebbins in Cambridge, Massachusetts, which contains a sheaf of Mount family letters originally collected by Charles J. Werner, the Long Island historian. All four assemblages of Mountiana are drawn upon in the pages that follow, and thanks are due all four for permission to use their material, very little of which has hitherto appeared in print. Since this catalogue provides the first published sampling in depth of the Mount manuscripts, its material has been selected with an eye toward providing a general overview of Mount's life, work, and attitudes in his own words and the words of those with whom he was most closely associated; excerpts from contemporary reviews have been omitted, however, (except in one rare instance wherein Mount quotes them himself) and this for two reasons. The first of these reasons is that we now possess an excessive quantity, in print, of contemporary statements of opinion about Mount.* The second and more important reason for our ignoring this contemporary opinion is that it merely tells us what the critics thought, which is often completely at variance with what Mount thought, and is only a shaky and problematical guide to what the public thought.

Some of the subjoined notes on Mount's paintings do not confine themselves to the specific

*See the following books:
  Bartlett Cowdrey and Hermann Warner Williams, Jr., *William Sidney Mount* (Columbia University Press, 1944).
  Neil Harris, *The Artist in American Society, the Formative Years, 1790-1860* (George Braziller, 1966).
  Lillian B. Miller, *Patrons and Patriotism, the Encouragement of the Fine Arts in the United States, 1790-1860* (University of Chicago Press, 1966).
  James T. Callow, *Kindred Spirits, Knickerbocker Writers and American Artists, 1807-1855* (University of North Carolina Press, 1967).

works from which they hang, but take off from the specific work to cast important sidelights on many aspects of the artist's career and achievement—his methods; his ideas about technique; his relations with collectors, publishers, merchants of art, and his own family; his views on life and art in general. In the following pages, then, catalogue and biography are combined.

Mount's casual spelling and haphazard punctuation have been preserved except where they would be misleading. One manuscript is quoted in nearly every entry below and so its title is abbreviated. The letters *MC* signify a document, preserved at the Suffolk Museum, which is headed *Catalogue of portraits and pictures painted by William Sidney Mount.* This is an extraordinarily complete and detailed list of the artist's works in his own hand; but, like all such lists, it is not *altogether* complete. (Incidentally, a "picture," in Mount's terminology, is a genre painting as opposed to a portrait.) The phrase *Whitney Journal* refers to a catch-all of jottings by Mount which was at one time in the library of the Whitney Museum of American Art and has been referred to by that title in some previous studies, although it is now part of the large collection at the Suffolk Museum.

The most important book in the Mount bibliography is *William Sidney Mount*, by Bartlett Cowdrey and Hermann Warner Williams, Jr., published for the Metropolitan Museum of Art by the Columbia University Press in 1944. At the time Cowdrey and Williams wrote, however, the major collections of Mount manuscripts had not been formed and, what is considerably more important, the collecting of Mount's paintings and drawings at the Suffolk Museum had only just begun.

It is astonishing to see how many of Mount's paintings which, according to Cowdrey and Williams, were sunk without a trace a quarter of a century ago are now among the holdings at Stony Brook. The Suffolk Museum possesses about three-quarters of the known pictures by Mount. The work of no other major American painter is so heavily concentrated in a single place. The Suffolk Museum owns so much primarily because it has discovered so much, thanks to the interest and generosity of Mr. and Mrs. Ward Melville, whose acquisition of Mounts and Mountiana for the public museum of his native town is one of the epics of American collecting.

ALFRED FRANKENSTEIN

San Francisco
August 1968

INTRODUCTION

"I was born in the village of Setauket—Long Island on the 26th of Nov. 1807. The first and most remarkable event of my life occurred when I was 6 or 7 months old. I was taken from my Mother (she being very sick) to be brought up by hand. I soon declined for want of proper or abundant nourishment and after several days was considered dead by my kind nurse, and tenderly laid away as so. My Father's sister being sent for to make further arrangements concerning me observed signs of life and immediately commenced nourishing me, she having a son about my own age—which act of charity soon restored me so far to life and strength that I might have been seen not many days after reaching for my great toe with all the enthusiasm of the infant in Raphael's Holy Family. From this period I remained I suppose much after the manner of other children, sometimes goodnatured and easily managed, sometimes the contrary. I was not always under the government or training of my Mother but alternately under the care of my Grandmother and herself until I was eight years old—when I went to New York to the care of my Uncle to be sent to school although I might have mentioned I attended school previous to this time in Stony Brook . . . "

Thus William Sidney Mount tells of himself in the first page of an autobiographical sketch.

William Sidney Mount, his brothers, Henry, Shepard and Robert, and their sister, Ruth, came to live in Stony Brook from Setauket, Long Island, a distance of some three miles, shortly after their father's death in 1814.

It was only natural that their mother, Julia, would come back to her father's house, a house built in 1757 by Eleazer Hawkins Jr. This house, later to become a National Landmark, and today owned by the Suffolk Museum, had, as was common in rural 19th Century America, one room turned into a post office and tavern, the interior of which is pictured in Mount's *California News*, *The Long Story*, *Sportsman's Last Visit* and *The Breakdown*.

All of Julia's sons were musical and artistic. One son, Robert, became a dancing teacher, the others artists, perhaps as a direct result of the influence of Julia's brother, Micah. Micah Hawkins, a New York store keeper who came to visit often in Stony Brook, was the composer of one of America's first musical comedies, *The Saw Mill or A Yankee Trick*, presented in New York in 1824.

William was also interested in music. He states in his diary: "I often ask someone to play while I am sketching for it livens the subject's face."

He exchanged fiddle tunes with Robert and patented several "improvements" in the violin. He was also fond of musical themes in his genre painting, as you will note in the exhibition. *Catching The Tune* shows his hollow-back violin.

As William stated, he went to New York to live and study with his uncle (Micah). He returned to Stony Brook, but by 1824 this 17-year-old boy was back in his brother Henry's sign-painting shop as an apprentice. During this stay in New York he spent many hours visiting the American Academy galleries and studying with Henry Inman, one of the leading portrait painters of the day. He wrote in his diary: "I preferred Mr. Inman's coloring and he was the only artist I would have staid with any length of time, but the fear of debt and the desire to be entirely original drove me from his Studio."

William returned home and in his catalogue of portraits he wrote: "In the year 1825 I commenced drawing with lead pencil and sometimes with white chalk in my brother's paint shop, No. 104 Cherry Street, New York.

"When I had a leisure moment, I did some scenes from Hamlet in umber and white. I believe a scene from Pericles, and in color a girl at the spring reading a love letter." ["Love letter" is stricken out and "ancient history" is inserted.]

"In the spring of 1828, at Stony Brook, I painted my first likeness." ["My first likeness" is stricken out and "a portrait of myself" is inserted.] "Directly after, I painted my first design, Christ Raising the Daughter of Jairus."

Christ Raising the Daughter of Jairus was his first entry in the annual exhibitions at the National Academy of Design. In 1830 he painted *The Country Dance*, his first genre picture. Comparing the "neoclassic" style and technique of his "first design" with those of his first genre painting, or contrasting the manner of his self-portrait of 1828 with the one of 1832 dramatically indicates the growth of this man's style. In less than four years, the "stilted crudeness" of his first approach evolved into a clarity of realization and a mastery of painterly techniques that were seldom equalled in American art of that day.

In 1831 he was elected an Associate of the National Academy of Design. In 1832 he was elected an Academician. At that time, Samuel F. B. Morse, the Academy's president, said, "William S. Mount will be regarded as one of the pioneers of American art." For nearly forty years after this, Mount contributed regularly to the Academy's annual exhibitions.

In the 1830's, Mount reached his first peak with such works as *The Sportsman's Last Visit*, *Farmers Nooning*, and *Raffling for a Goose*.

His work, viewed in conjunction with his letters and diaries, reveals a highly complex individual, full of puzzling contradictions and inconsistencies. He was the first to give the Negro a place of dignity in American painting, but he was an ardent member of the Democratic Party, fought the Abolitionists, and called the Republicans "Lincolnpoops." In his diary William reflects, "I must paint such pictures as speak at once to the spectator, scenes that are most popular, that will be understood on the instant," but shortly thereafter he notes, "I must not allow myself to be driven from portraits into the picture line." Throughout his life there was conflict between his desire to paint such scenes and his desire to excel as a portraitist.

Although he is justly celebrated as America's first important genre painter, his diary contains not one word of comment about people or the observation of daily life; but he fills page upon page with formulas for pigments and media, their preparation and application. When he is in the country his journals criticize the rural life; as soon as he goes to the city, he is appalled by conditions and hurries back to Stony Brook.

One day Mount will write: "Never paint for the few, paint for the many—painting familiar objects has the advantage over writing, for you can address yourself to all—it is not necessary to be gifted in languages to understand a painting—if the story is well told." And the next day he will insist: "I must endeavour to follow the bent of my own inclinations, to paint large or small, grave or gay as I please. Not to be dictated to by others. Every artist should know his own powers and act accordingly."

In the later diaries of William Sidney Mount, many entries show concern about techniques, his personal habits and his health, indicating more and more time given over to thought and less spent in the execution of finished works: "... there is a difficulty in getting down to painting, the temptation to delay is great." "It must be the spirit of opposition that torments me when I think of my duty." "I cannot paint anything unless I fully understand it." "Thank God I am temperate. I am getting along in years and must attach myself to nature." "I must study nature and endeavour to capture it or I can never paint it again." "I must have long intervals from painting—perhaps it is wrong to put off from day to day. Rest and reflection seem like food to me."

In the 1860's he drove around the countryside in a portable studio that he designed to shield him from the weather and protect his failing health. The portable studio practically became his home and much of his last sketching was done there. His notes show that he planned to do far more than he accomplished; never again did he show the spirit of the 1830's and 40's. But he kept on painting and writing even after the shock of his brother Shepard's death in September of '68.

That fall he left the house at Stony Brook, where he had lived so long, and went back to live in Setauket with his brother, Nelson. He died suddenly on the 19th of November, 1868.

This exhibition opens at the National Gallery of Art almost a hundred years to the day since his death. The exhibition is one in a biennial series at the National Gallery devoted to major American painters. It seems only fitting that our present tribute to William Sidney Mount should include him with Copley and Stuart, Eakins and Homer, as a link between the artists of those two eras.

Jane des Grange, *Director*
SUFFOLK MUSEUM AND CARRIAGE HOUSE

1. CHRIST RAISING THE DAUGHTER OF JAIRUS

1828

Oil on panel, 18¼ x 24⅜ in.

SUFFOLK MUSEUM AND CARRIAGE HOUSE, MELVILLE COLLECTION, STONY BROOK, LONG ISLAND

MC: "In the spring of 1828 I painted my first likeness. A portrait of myself. Directly after, I painted my first design, 'Christ Raising the Daughter of Jairus.'"

In another document, undated (SM 0.11.3549), Mount says, "Among my first compositions were The Daughter of Jairus. The President [of the National Academy of Design] S.F.B. Morse remarked as respects composition he had not seen its equal amongst any of the modern masters."

According to the Gospel of St. Luke, Chapter 8, Jairus was "a ruler of the synagogue," who besought Jesus to visit his daughter, who was twelve years of age and was dying. A messenger from the house of Jairus reported, indeed, that the child was already dead. Jesus went, nevertheless, to the house, "And he put them all out, and took her by the hand, and called, saying, Maid, arise. And her spirit came again, and she arose straightway: and he commanded to give her meat. And her parents were astonished; but he charged them that they should tell no man what was done."

2. SAUL AND THE WITCH OF ENDOR

1828

Oil on canvas, 36 x 48 in.

NATIONAL COLLECTION OF FINE ARTS, SMITHSONIAN INSTITUTION
GIFT OF INTERNATIONAL BUSINESS MACHINES CORPORATION

MC: "My second design Saul and the Witch of Endor. Size of the picture, three by four feet. Painted in New York. Sold to T. Bailey, Esq. for $20.00."

The First Book of Kings tells us how Saul, fearing to lose his kingdom to the Philistines, went to a woman of Endor "who had a familiar spirit" and ordered her to raise up the ghost of the prophet Samuel. She did so, but Saul had no comfort from Samuel's words; the prophet rebuked him sternly and predicted his defeat and death.

"T. Bailey, Esq.", who bought this picture from Mount for twenty dollars, was the renowned Navy officer, Theodorus Bailey (1805-1877), whose portrait Mount was to paint (for seventy-five dollars) in October, 1852. Shortly thereafter, on December 28, 1852, Bailey wrote Mount as follows:

"The Painting of the Witch of Endor raising Samuel which I purchased of you some years since has to me a peculiar value as one of the early fruits of your genius. But I would like to have from you an account of your first efforts at drawing, Colouring, Shading, and Painting. What induced you to turn your attention to Historic painting, the History of the painting in my possession, with a narrative of the circumstances, trials, troubles, advantages, and disadvantages and encouragements which you met with in painting this one of your earliest pictures, and why you abandoned the Historic Style for the one in which you have become so eminent. In short I want a brief history of your life as connected with painting . . . Your portrait of me is very much admired. . . ."

To this Mount replied, on January 5, 1853:

"Your kind note requesting me to furnish you with materials of myself 'as connected with painting' . . . Now Capt. that is asking a little too much—why it would take me three months to shell it all out—to clean the cob all off, and who would feed me with pudding and milk all that while.

"Echo answers who."

"I am pleased that your portrait is so much admired—I will call and see you when I visit the City—"

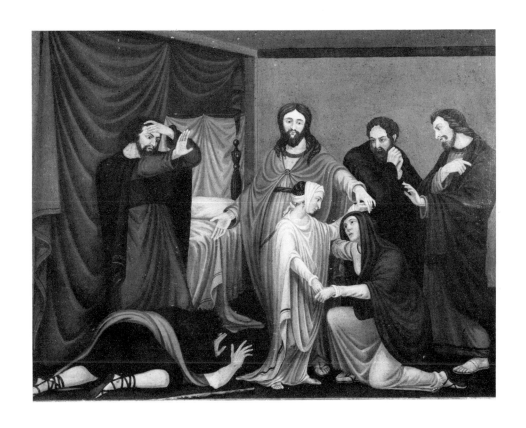

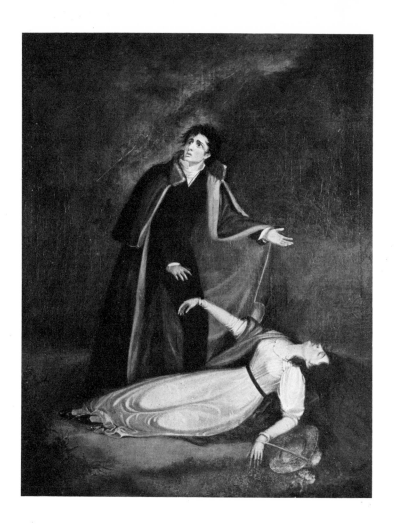

3. CELADON AND AMELIA

1829

Oil on canvas, 24 x 20 in.

SUFFOLK MUSEUM AND CARRIAGE HOUSE, MELVILLE COLLECTION, STONY BROOK, LONG ISLAND

MC: "Year 1829. 'Celadon and Amelia,' from Thomson's Seasons. Painted in New York...... $19.00"

The story of Celadon and Amelia occurs in the "Summer" section of James Thomson's *The Seasons,* published in 1727. Most of this section is given over to an idyllic picture of July and August, with their hay-making, sheep-shearing, swimming, and so on, but in order to indicate the perils of nature even at this time of the year, Thomson tells how Amelia was struck by lightning and killed while walking with her lover, Celadon.

When Mount's painting was exhibited at the National Academy of Design in 1829, the catalogue contained the following lines from Thomson:

> " . . . From his void embrace,
> Mysterious Heaven! that moment to the ground,
> A blackened corpse, was struck the beauteous maid.
> But who can paint the lover as he stood,
> Pierc'd by severe amazement, hating life,
> Speechless, and fix'd, in all the death of woe!"

4. JULIA ANN HAWKINS MOUNT

1830

Oil on canvas, 30 x 24¾ in.

SUFFOLK MUSEUM AND CARRIAGE HOUSE, MELVILLE COLLECTION, STONY BROOK, LONG ISLAND

MC: "Year 1830 . . . Portrait of My Mother, painted at Stony Brook, Long Island."

Diary, November 24, 1864: "Twenty-three years ago my dear Mother died. I often think of her." Mount painted a replica of this portrait in 1855.

5. RUSTIC DANCE AFTER A SLEIGH RIDE

1830

Oil on canvas, 22 x 27¼ in.

MUSEUM OF FINE ARTS, BOSTON, M. AND M. KAROLIK COLLECTION

MC: "Year 1830 . . . Rustic Dance painted at Stony Brook. When painting it I used a chair for an easel while the carpenter was making me one. In the possession of E. Windust Esq. N.Y. $30.00."

This is Mount's earliest surviving genre painting. According to his own catalogue of his works, he had previously painted two others—*A Girl at the Spring Reading a Love Letter,* apparently done in 1828, and *Girl with a Pitcher Standing at a Well,* painted in the following year. Both of these pictures are lost. Both must have been in a quietly sentimental vein and altogether unlike the vigorously anecdotal Mount who was born with *The Rustic Dance.*

In the month of October, 1830, the American Institute of the City of New-York held its third annual trade fair at the Masonic Hall. The American Institute was a protectionist organization, and in its catalogue it listed the duties that would have to be paid, in each instance, on comparable imported goods. Painting and sculpture provided one of the numerous categories of the fair; according to the catalogue, they were protected by a tariff of fifteen percent. Mount won first prize with *The Rustic Dance* at this exhibition. (Quidor and the Broweres, father and son, won lesser awards; the names of the judges are unknown.)

The "Buy American" atmosphere of the fair doubtless had much to do with the great hit which *The Rustic Dance* very clearly made. This success seems to have established Mount's reputation at a single stroke and to have solidified the interest in rural American genre subjects which he was to pursue for the rest of his life.

The artist himself was astonished at the success he achieved with this picture, painted less than two years after his first, tentative efforts and at a time when his total tally of completed work amounted barely to two dozen canvases. On May 29, 1830, he wrote from New York to his brother Nelson as follows:

"I have plenty of Business. I am painting the Portraits of the Rev. Mr. Underdonk and Mr. Thompson, the Architect &c. I shall be up home as soon as I paint 3 or 4 more to Paint some landskapes from nature, my Contra Dance atracts a great deal of attention, I will give you a coppy of a Critic on the Pictures, he blows them up like fun, we cant find him out, Published in Paphlet form—

"Mounts little girl from Cottage comes;
  In Natures tints she lovely blooms,
  Whilst o'er her head the willow tree
  Waves as it should so droopingly.

"He leads us up a Rustic Dance,
  Such things are better done in France,
  But this shall keep no under station,
  It shows some scenes within the nation.

"Take nature for a guide and she
  Will show what wants variety—
  Study good composition well,
  One day in this thou may'st excel.

"In harmony more thy collors blend,
  I speak as t'were to any friend,
  Who leaves them now in hopes to se
  Still better things next year from the.

"Wrote in a hurry, burn up my letter."

The Suffolk Museum possesses a one-page manuscript, apparently not a letter, diary-entry, or portion of an autobiographical sketch, wherein Mount sets down the following incident:

"One cool day in 1830, as I was engaged in painting 'The Country Dance,' in an upper south room— the sun was gentle and I thought it warm enough—not so, thought my Grand Mother for in she came with a large iron kettle (such as the yankees use to bake pumpkin bread with) and glowing with hot coals, and said 'Wᵐ. I have thought since you would paint by this light that some coals would warm the room, for it is quite a cold day.' I thanked her kindly and worked away. My thoughts were busy with the figures in my picture, when presently I began to yawn, to feel sleepy, but I roused (?) up in my chair & worked on. All at once I felt still more heavy & stupid—my hand and brush, palette and maulstick caught the infection. My chin settled upon my bosom like one going to sleep—There before

14

me on the easel stood a group moving in the dance full of mirth and hilarity while death stood over my chair ready to graspe the painter—but my good spirit whispered in my ear and my eyes moved slowly around the room. The cause of my strange feelings struck me like a ray of light. I saw the kettle of charcoal. I gathered all my strength [*illegible*] the door and opened it with difficulty and I was save. Elliott the painter was caught in the same trap."

The final document in the case of *The Rustic Dance* is a letter which Mount wrote from Stony Brook to one Martin E. Thompson on October 10, 1841, eleven years after the picture had won its prize at the fair:

"I see by the papers that you are one of the managers of the American Institute in the City of New York. I have therefore thought it proper to request you to lay the following before the Board of Managers for the Institute.

"I received from the Fair of the American Institute in the City of New York Oct. 1830 the first Premium for a painting representing a Country or Rustic Dance. I was told by the Secy. that If I paid two dollars I should be presented with a Silver Medal, but instead of the Medal, I was sent a Diploma. I value the latter, but I should value the Medal still more."

In connection with this painting, one might well point out that dancing and fiddling played major roles in the lives of the Mount brothers. Nelson was a dancing teacher by profession and William was an expert fiddler who drastically redesigned the violin. The extensive correspondence between Nelson and William deals in great detail with the figures of country dances, and the two constantly exchanged fiddle tunes. William's use of the musicians' term *Contredanse* in the above-quoted letter to Nelson is significant, even if William, like so many since his time, misunderstands the etymology and root meaning of the word and spells it *Contra Dance*.

6. DANCING ON THE BARN FLOOR

1831

Oil on canvas, 25 x 30 in.

SUFFOLK MUSEUM AND CARRIAGE HOUSE, MELVILLE COLLECTION, STONY BROOK, LONG ISLAND

MC: "Year 1831 . . . Interior of a barn with figures dancing. Part of the foreground unfinished. Size of the picture 25 by 30 in. Sold in 1835 to James H. Patterson Esq N.Y. $111.00."

Patterson is mentioned, also, in the following highly characteristic diary entry for January 1, 1848:

"A new year is always welcome. I feel thankful for past favors. I spent part of today in the village of Huntington, & Stony Brook. A friend—Mr. Curtis—advised me not to bury my talents in so retired a place as Stony Brook, but to travel. I had done well but could do better &c.—Mr. Patterson said that I lacked ambition, should travel to foreign parts, &c. I can find nature everywhere. White scumbled over flesh after it has been strongly painted has a good effect."

7. PORTRAIT OF A WOMAN

1832

Oil on canvas, 30 x 25 in.

SUFFOLK MUSEUM AND CARRIAGE
HOUSE, MELVILLE COLLECTION, STONY
BROOK, LONG ISLAND

MC at this time lists numerous paintings as
Portrait of a Lady, Lady and Gentleman, and
so on, but the identity of the sitters has been
totally lost.

8. MRS. TIMOTHY STARR

1833

Oil on canvas, 30 x 25 in.

SUFFOLK MUSEUM AND CARRIAGE
HOUSE, MELVILLE COLLECTION, STONY
BROOK, LONG ISLAND

According to Mr. and Mrs. Hallock W. Beals,
who presented this portrait to the Suffolk
Museum in 1942, Mrs. Starr was born Mary
Fosdick in Middletown, Connecticut, on May
13, 1758, and married Timothy Starr on
August 20, 1780. The date of her death is apparently not recorded.

9. THE SPORTSMAN'S LAST VISIT

1835

Oil on canvas, 21½ x 17½ in.

SUFFOLK MUSEUM AND CARRIAGE HOUSE, MELVILLE COLLECTION, STONY BROOK, LONG ISLAND

MC: "Year 1835 . . . Sportsman's Last Visit, on canvas, 17 in by 21 in. and the Studious Boy. Sold to George P. Morris Esq. for $100."

Whitney Journal, November 14, 1852: "Bar-room scene—22 x 27 in. painted in Setauket in 1835 at the house of Gen. Satterlee by the aid of two south windows in winter and separated by a curtain to divide the two lights. The artist by one window & the model by the other—Sportsman's Last Visit—done at the same time and by the same light. Courtship or Winding Up painted in the same way—at Stony Brook at the residence of Capt. Henry Smith. The Raffle and Tough Story were painted by using two windows . . ."

The name of George P. Morris recurs several times in the Mount documents, most notably as the recipient of a long, bitter tirade against the American Art-Union which Mount sent him on December 3, 1848. According to Mount, this famous lottery was run by ignoramuses for their own profit; he accuses them of sharp practice and other misdemeanors, and he participated in various rival schemes for the distribution of art largely, one suspects, out of a desire to get even with the Art-Union for its real or suspected mistreatment of him. Since the American Art-Union is one of the sacred cows of American art history, it is refreshing to find a dissenting view of it so forcefully expressed by so distinguished an artist. We provide the full text of the letter to Morris in our notes on *Loss and Gain.* Mount ultimately made his peace with the Art-Union, however, as witness our notes on *The Novice.*

10. FARMERS NOONING

1836

Oil on canvas, 20 x 24 in.

SUFFOLK MUSEUM AND CARRIAGE HOUSE, MELVILLE COLLECTION, STONY BROOK, LONG ISLAND

MC: "Year 1836 . . . Farmers nooning. Size of the canvas 20 x 24 in. painted for

Frame	30.00
Mr. Jonathan Sturges, N.Y.	$270.00
Picture and frame	300.00

"It has been engraved."

Mount to Benjamin F. Thompson, historian of Long Island, December 31, 1848:

" . . . As long ago as 1836, when I was painting the Farmers nooning, my late brother H.S. Mount handed me a piece of native umber found in the banks near this place and desired me to make use of it in my picture. I did so and found it as he had represented, transparent, and a good dryer. I have used it more or less ever since and find it a valuable pigment. It looks lighter and makes a cooler tint when burnt, directly opposite to Turkey Umber. In the gradations of flesh with white it is truly delightful. It unites harmoniously with all colors. It should be ground in nut or raw linseed oil. . . ."

Whitney Journal, November 14, 1852: "Farmer Husking Corn, painted in 1833 in the open air—the canopy of heaven for my paint room—Studious Boy in the same way—Farmers bargaining painted out of doors—Undutiful Boys also—Boy Hoeing Corn—in the open air—Cider Making painted on the spot, also, the Farmers Nooning . . ."

Jonathan Sturges (1802-1874) was one of the most important collectors of American art during Mount's lifetime. He was a partner in the wholesale grocery business of the still more famous collector, Luman Reed, and one of the leaders in the move to form a public museum out of Reed's collection after its owner's death in 1836. This museum, the New York Art Gallery, opened in 1844; it was the first public art museum in New York, and according to Neil Harris (*The Artist in American Society*, 1966) it was one of the three major art associations in that city in its time. (The others were the National Academy of Design and the American Art-Union.) Mount donated his painting now called *Fortune Telling* to the New York Gallery in 1846; this must have been one of the very few additions to the hundred-odd paintings inherited from Luman Reed to be made to the collection of the New York Gallery during the fourteen years of its existence. Eventually, says Lillian Miller (*Patrons and Patriotism*, 1966) the public grew tired of seeing the same old things over and over again and Sturges tired of making up the deficit of the institution; consequently the collection was donated in 1858 to the New-York Historical Society, in whose galleries it remains to this day.

Mount painted three pictures for Sturges and was his close friend for more than twenty years. In addition to *Farmers Nooning*, Sturges owned *Ringing the Pig* (1842) and *Who'll Turn the Grindstone* (1851). The two men discussed several ideas for pictures in letters which passed between them in 1837 and 1839, but nothing, apparently, came of this exchange.

On April 15, 1851, William Sidney Mount arose at the annual supper of the National Academy of Design and made the following speech, a copy of which he entered in his diary:

"Mr. President, it is our duty to speak on all occasions of the men that adorn their walls with pictures rather than with looking glasses. I would particularize at this time one gentleman known to you all. Since the death of Luman Reed, no man in this city holds a more prominent place in the affections of artists and the public than our esteemed President of the New York Gallery, Jonathan Sturges. He has apartments richly decorated with paintings and busts by native artists, and I believe has but one mirror, which reflects well his taste. He reminds me of some of our good old farmers. I know him to be one by the fact that I have *sanded his rifle, rung his hogs,* and *turned his grindstone.*"

The "rifle" to which Mount refers here is not a gun but the scythe sharpener in the hands of the seated man at the extreme left in *Farmers Nooning*.

11. WINDING UP

1836

Oil on panel, 18⅜ x 15 in.

MR. AND MRS. MALCOLM E. SMITH, NEW YORK CITY

MC: "Year 1836 . . . Courtship, or winding up. It represents a young Lady winding while her lover is holding a skein of yarn. Painted for John Glover Esq. Size of the mahogany pannel, 15 by 19 ½ inches. $200.00"

The present owner of the picture, Mrs. Malcolm E. Smith, is the granddaughter of John Glover of Fairfield, Connecticut, for whom it was painted.

(Also see notes on *The Sportsman's Last Visit.*)

12. THE LONG STORY

1837

Oil on canvas, 17 x 22 in.

THE CORCORAN GALLERY OF ART, WASHINGTON, D.C.

MC: "Year 1837 . . . Tough Story. Painted for Mr. Robert Gilmor of Baltimore Size of the picture I belive was 17 x 21 inches, and painted on Mahogany.

"Price of picture		200.00
do	frame	22.00
do	packing	2.00
		$224.00"

Robert Gilmor of Baltimore was, like Luman Reed and Jonathan Sturges, a wealthy business man who collected much American art. A letter of Mount's to him, dated August 20, 1836, indicates that Gilmor had seen Mount's *Bargaining for a Horse* and *Truant Gamblers* in Reed's gallery and had written Mount asking him if he would accept a commission, the subject to be left entirely to the artist to select.

Mount waited well over a year before fulfilling Gilmor's commission. On December 5, 1837, he wrote Gilmor the most elaborately "literary" and programmatic description of a painting which he ever put down on paper:

"Your letter of 25th ult. I have recd containing a check for $224. I thank you for it. such promptitude adds value to the amount.

"Yours of the 29th I have also recd, fulfilling the promise of the preceding as giving your opinion of the picture and I am happy to find with but a slight difference your impressions of my intentions are what I intended them. The man puffing out his smoke is a regular built Long Island tavern and store keeper, who amongst us is often a Gen. or Judge, or Postmaster, or what you please as regards standing in society and as you say has quite the air of a citizen.

"The man standing wrapt in his cloak is a traveller as you supposed and is in no way connected with the rest only waiting the arrival of the stage, he appears to be listening to what the old man is saying. I designed the picture as a conversation piece. The principal interest to be centered in the old invalid who certainly talks with much zeal. I have placed him in a particular chair which he is always supposed to claim by right of possession, being but seldom out of it from the rising to the going down of the sun. A kind of bar-room oracle, chief umpire during all seasons of warm debate whether religious, moral, or political, and first taster of every new barrel of cider rolled in the cellar, a glass of which he now holds in his hand while he is entertaining his young landlord with the longest story he is ever supposed to tell, having fairly tired out every other frequenter of the establishment.

"I agree with you in the opinion that it is my most finished performance."

23

13. RAFFLING FOR THE GOOSE

1837

Oil on panel, 17 x 23 ⅛ in.

THE METROPOLITAN MUSEUM OF ART, NEW YORK, N.Y.,
GIFT OF JOHN D. CRIMMINS, 1897

MC: "Year 1837 . . . The raffle. Painted for Mr. Henry Brevoort of N. York. Size of the picture 17⅛ by 23⅛ in. painted on mahogany. Price of the raffle $300. He gave me three hundred, said I did not charge enough." *Footnote:* "Price of the raffle 250. Mr. Brevoort kindly gave me 50 dollars extra."

Whitney Journal, December 26, 1849: "When I painted the Raffle in the winter of 1837 I used to walk over to my paint room and make fire before breakfast. I must do the same at this date 1849 & 50. To prevent my plate of paints from freezing I must take it every night to my place of boarding. I live with my sister, Mrs. Ruth H. Seabury."

Whitney Journal, November 14, 1852: "The Raffle and Tough Story were painted by using two windows." (For the context of this remark, see notes on *The Sportsman's Last Visit*.)

15.   THE PAINTER'S TRIUMPH

1838

Oil on canvas, 19½ x 23½ in.

THE PENNSYLVANIA ACADEMY OF THE FINE ARTS

MC: "Year 1838 . . . Artist showing his own work, painted for E.L. Carey Esq of Philadelphia. It was engraved for the Gift. Painted on mahogany. Price of the picture   250.00

frame and box   24.00

$274.00"

Diary, July 21, 1838: "I am painting a picture representing a painter showing his picture to a country man—farmer. It is thought to be my best."

E.L. Carey of Philadelphia was editor of *The Gift*, one of those fancy Christmas annuals which were so popular during the nineteenth century. He owned four Mounts; in addition to *The Painter's Triumph* he had *Boys Bird Egging, The Disagreeable Surprise,* and *The Deadfall*. His typesetters could presumably decipher his handwriting; if so, they were more perceptive readers than the compiler of this catalogue. He seems to have given Mount instructions for packing and shipping *The Painter's Triumph* on August 31, 1838, and to have acknowledged its receipt, with great pleasure, on September 11. On December 21, 1839, he asked Mount if he had a painting available for loan to The Gift for the following year's edition. Mount replied, on December 29:

"The Gift as a volume I think very favorably of.—I must acknowledge that one of my pictures, Farmers Bargaining is not as well engraved as I should have liked although the engraver assured me that he would do it as well as the price and time at which he was limited would allow. It is my opinion that in so conspicuous a place as an Annual the engraver if he accepts of a job should do his very best let the price be what it may.

14.   JEDEDIAH WILLIAMSON

1836

Oil on panel, 16 x 13 in.

SUFFOLK MUSEUM AND CARRIAGE HOUSE, MELVILLE COLLECTION, STONY BROOK, LONG ISLAND

MC: "Year 1837 . . . I made a sketch of Col. Williamson's son after he was killed by a loaded waggon passing over his body. A portrait. $15.00"

Painting portraits of the dead, and especially of dead children, was part of every artist's stock-in-trade in nineteenth century America. Mount repeatedly painted such portraits, but he seldom did so without recording a protest against the practice. Thus, in his catalogue for the year 1846 he makes the following entry: "Portrait of Rev. Charles Seabury, painted after death from memory for his son Rev. Samuel Seabury D.D. I only charged him twenty dollars. And the last I hope I shall paint after death. Death is a patron to some painters, I had rather paint the living."

Later entries on the same theme run as follows: " . . . A portrait of Frances Amelia Moubray, $50.00 — after death. Death incourages the fine arts." "For portraits after death I must charge double price & be careful how I strain my eyes by painting after Daguerrotypes." But it was not always a matter of copying photographs; Mount observes that one advantage the painter has over the photographer is that the painter can remember the faces of dead people.

Much as Mount disliked painting likenesses of the dead, he could never dispense with that aspect of his art. The necrological aspects of his profession may have had something to do with Mount's strong interest in spiritualism; the only person who could bring back the dead more dramatically than the painter was the medium.

16. MIRIAM WEEKS UNDERHILL

1838

Oil on canvas, 27 x 34 in.

SUFFOLK MUSEUM AND CARRIAGE HOUSE, MELVILLE COLLECTION, STONY BROOK, LONG ISLAND

MC: "Year 1838 . . . Three portraits of Mrs. Meriam Weeks and one portrait of Miss Meriam Underhill Oyster Bay Long Island, $200.00."

17. CATCHING RABBITS

1839

Oil on panel, 18 x 21 in.

SUFFOLK MUSEUM AND CARRIAGE HOUSE, MELVILLE COLLECTION, STONY BROOK, LONG ISLAND

MC: "Year 1839. Boys trapping or Catching Rabbits, painted for Charles A. Davis, N. York—on mahogany—size 21½ by 18 inches. Price of the picture $250.

"In the fall of 1839, most of my time was taken up by sketching from nature with a lead pencil."

(This is the entire entry in the catalogue for 1839.)

The Suffolk Museum possesses the manuscript, not in Mount's handwriting, of an article, copied from an unknown source, stating that William Schaus came to the United States from Paris in 1847 as agent for the print-publishing house of Goupil, Vibert and Company, that he was much impressed with Mount's painting, *The Power of Music*, and forthwith arranged to have it published by his firm. "This was the first recognition of American Art by Europe," says the unknown author, "for Mr. Mount's picture was the first one ever sent to Paris to be engraved." The article goes on to list five more Mounts published by Goupil, Vibert and Company thanks to Schaus. They were *Music Is Contagious*, now known as *Dance of the Haymakers*, *Boys Catching Rabbits*, *Just in Tune*, *Right and Left*, and *Raffling for a Goose*, now known as *The Lucky Throw*.* The last two paintings, according to the anonymous author, were directly commissioned by Schaus, which is interesting, because they were both portraits of Negroes, and Schaus was later to commission two more Negro portraits from Mount, *The Banjo Player* and *The Bones Player*. Since all these pictures were reproduced in Paris primarily for sale in Europe, they provide a most instructive insight into European attitudes toward the United States in the middle of the nineteenth century. The statement that the engraving of *The Power of Music* "was the first recognition of American Art by Europe" is, of course, an exaggeration, but the Goupil engravings of paintings by Mount established a reputation for our artist abroad at a time when American art as a whole was ignored outside this country; what they did for European stereotypes regarding American life can only be conjectured.

Schaus took up residence in New York as Goupil's agent. He and Mount became firm friends, and the correspondence between them was very extensive for a period of six years. The earliest surviving example of that correspondence is a letter from Mount to "Messieurs Goupil, Vibert & Co.," dated December 13, 1848:

"I am delighted that you intend to have in New York City a perpetual free Gallery to improve the public taste. One of the great emjoyments of life is in looking at paintings & engravings—they kill time so profitably. I hope all the friends of the Fine Arts in this Country will become members of your 'International Art-Union.' Your plan is an interesting one of having from France 'a school of art and artists'—also, of sending an American Student abroad to study modern and ancient art. I encourage the hope I may be selected as one of the Students, to be sent to Europe to study art and nature. I intend to be a subscriber to your magnificent project, when I go to the city."

There is more here than meets the casual eye, since the Goupil-Schaus International Art-Union was to be set up in direct competition to the American Art-Union; and this letter was written exactly ten days after Mount's tirade against the American Art-Union which we publish in our notes on *Loss and Gain*. Mount must have known that he could not qualify for one of the International Art-Union's

---

*Changes in the titles of Mount's paintings are the cause of endless confusion in the literature, but this is the most confusing instance of all because there is another, earlier, painting by Mount also entitled *Raffling for a Goose*. This particular mixup seems to have originated with Schaus himself, which suggests that the anonymous article was inspired if not written by him.

European scholarships because the announcement thereof, published on December 11 and quite obviously the springboard for his letter, stated that they were limited to candidates under twenty-five years of age; he was forty-one.

Mount to Charles Lanman, January 8, 1850: . . . "However, as you request, I will mention with pleasure two or three of my last pieces—'Turning the Leaf,' 'Farmer Whetting His Scythe,' 'The Well by the Wayside,' and 'Just in Tune.' The last represents a character tuning his violin—the size of life—on canvass 25 x 30. It is to be published by Goupil Vibert and Co. and has gone to Paris to be engraved by the celebrated Emile Lasalle. 'Boys Trapping,' painted for Charles A. Davis of N.Y. City in 1839 it is now in Paris under the magic hand of Leon Noel and then both of the above paintings after serving the purposes of the engraver are to be exhibited in the ensuing collection of paintings at the Tuilleries . . ."

Smithtown Diary, Volume I, Page 9 (1855?): "G.H. Warren Esq Mount Ida, Troy, N. York owns the Boys Catching Rabbits."

19. CIDER MAKING

1841

Oil on canvas, 27 x 34⅛ in.

THE METROPOLITAN MUSEUM OF ART, NEW YORK, N. Y.,
CHARLES ALLEN MUNN BEQUEST, 1966

MC: "Year 1841. Cider making, painted for Mr. Charles A. Davis N. York—received two hundred and fifty dollars for the picture. Size of the canvass 27 in by 34 inches."

Mount to Benjamin F. Thompson, December 5, 1840: " . . . I have a picture on the esel I think you would be pleased to see. The subject is cider making in the old way. I feel in the spirit of painting and have plenty to do . . . "

Robert Nelson Mount to William Sidney, January 17, 1841: " . . . I think your last picture, 'Cider Making,' should have been painted large and placed in one of the vacant squares at the Government House in Washington City . . . "

Whitney Journal, Page 123: " . . . Cider making, painted on the spot . . . "

On April 14, 1841, the *New York American* published a detailed description of this painting wherein its separate visual incidents are transformed into the successive episodes of a short story. This story, which is indicative of the over-riding stress on narrative characteristic of the criticism of Mount's time (but not at all characteristic of Mount's own views and intentions) is reproduced in full in Stuart P. Feld's article, "In the Midst of 'High Vintage,'" with which the Metropolitan signalized its recent acquisition of the painting. (Metropolitan Museum of Art Bulletin, April, 1967, Pages 292-307.) This is incomparably the finest article on Mount ever written.

18. BOY HOEING CORN

1840

Oil on panel, 14 x 11 in.

SUFFOLK MUSEUM AND CARRIAGE HOUSE, MELVILLE COLLECTION, STONY BROOK,
LONG ISLAND

MC: "Year 1840 . . . Boy hoeing Corn, size 15 in. by 11⅝ inches. painted on wood. Sold to Hon. Aaron
Ward May 1841 for $100."

Whitney Journal, Page 123: " . . . Boy hoeing corn painted in the open air . . . "

Aaron Ward was a member of Congress who was much interested in fostering American art, especially
by employing native painters to produce murals for the Capitol. (See Lillian Miller, *Patrons and Patriotism*, Page 52.)

20. RINGING THE PIG

1842

Oil on canvas, 25 x 30 in.

NEW YORK STATE HISTORICAL ASSOCIATION, COOPERSTOWN

MC: "Year 1842. Scene in a Long Island Farm-Yard. Painted on canvas 25 x 30 in. For Jon[a]. Sturges
Esq. He liberally paid me thirty dollars more than I asked him for the picture. He gave me $300.00. The
picture cost him altogether $337.00."

For Sturges, see the entry on *Farmers Nooning*.

33

21. GIRL ASLEEP

1843

Oil on canvas, 21 x 36 in.

SUFFOLK MUSEUM AND CARRIAGE HOUSE, MELVILLE COLLECTION, STONY BROOK,
LONG ISLAND

MC: "In the spring of 1843 I painted a girl asleep. The size of canvas I blieve 22 by 27 in. Not sold.
Present to my niece Maria Seabury."

Charles Lanman to Mount, February 27, 1844: " . . . How comes on that beautiful little sleeping
creature of your pencil? My first impression of that picture was not very favorable but now I think
it a fine thing and my attachment to it is that of a lover. I suppose you'll have it at the Academy? . . ."

Diary, December 23, 1847: "In my picture of a Girl asleep the shadows of the face should have been
cooler, the mass of light being warm."

22. THE DEAD FALL or TRAP SPRUNG

1844

Oil on panel, 13 x 17 in.

SUFFOLK MUSEUM AND CARRIAGE HOUSE, MELVILLE COLLECTION, STONY BROOK,
LONG ISLAND

MC: "In the year 1844 . . . one picture (Trap Sprung) painted for E.L. Carey Esqr. received 125 dollars
size 13 in by 17 on panel."

Mount to Charles Lanman, March 11, 1844: " . . . I have lately painted a picture for E.L. Carey Esqr.
called Trap sprung, a snow scene. Mr. Carey liked it so well that he gave me a commission to paint
another to be called summer . . . "

For Carey, see notes on *The Painter's Triumph.*

23. DANCE OF THE HAYMAKERS

1845

Oil on canvas, 25 x 30 in.

SUFFOLK MUSEUM AND CARRIAGE HOUSE, MELVILLE COLLECTION, STONY BROOK, LONG ISLAND

MC: "Stony Brook, 1845. April 10th One picture Dance of the Haymakers painted for Charles M. Leupp. Price two hundred—he generously paid me twenty five dollars more than my charge. On canvass 25 by 30 in." (The title *Dance of the Haymakers* is lightly crossed out in this entry and the alternative title, *Music is Contagious*, is written above it.)

Mount to Leupp, March 11, 1845: "I am pleased to say that the order you so kindly gave me has interested my feelings for some time. You have waited with great patience and I sincerely hope that the picture will have sufficient merit to pay you for the delay.

"The size of the picture is 25 in by 30 in. I have a quarter of an inch moulding around it to preserve the edges, and at the same time when it is framed to show the whole surface of the painting. This you will mention to the frame makers. I am quite desirous to exhibit the picture if agreeable to you. I think I can get it done on time. Therefore I have written early that you may order the frame accordingly. The Academy receives pictures up the 5th of April."

Leupp—who was a leather merchant and one of the most important collectors of European and American art then in New York—replied on the following day: " . . . I have no objection that you exhibit the picture and shall immediately order the frame agreeable to your directions."

24. EEL SPEARING AT SETAUKET

1845

Oil on canvas, 29 x 36 in.

NEW YORK STATE HISTORICAL ASSOCIATION, COOPERSTOWN

MC: "1845 . . . One picture, Fishing along shore, painted for George W. Strong Esqr. On canvas 29 x 36. He paid me two hundred and fifty dollars." *Footnote:* "Recollections of early days. Fishing along shore —with a view of the Hon Selah B. Strong's residence in the distance during a drought at Setauket, Long Island."

Mount to Charles Lanman, November 17, 1847: "An old Negro by the name of Hector gave me the first lesson in spearing flat-fish & eels. Early one morning we were along shore according to appointment, it was calm, and the water was as clear as a mirror, every object perfectly distinct to the depth from one to twelve feet, now and then could be seen an eel darting through the seaweed or a flatfish shifting his place and throwing the sand over his body for safty. 'Steady there at the stern,' said Hector, as he stood on the bow (with his spear held ready) looking into the element with all the philosophy of a Crane, while I would watch his motions, and move the boat according to the direction of his spear. 'Slow now, we are coming on the ground,' on sandy and gravelly bottoms are found the best fish— 'look out for the eyes' observes Hector, as he hauls in a flatfish, out of his bed of gravel, 'he will grease the pan, my boy,' as the fish makes the water fly about in the boat. The old negro mutters to himself with a great deal of satisfaction 'fine day—not a cloud—we will make old mistress laugh—now creep— in fishing you must learn to creep,' as he kept hauling in the flat-fish and eels, right and left, with his quick and unering hand—'Stop the boat,' shouts Hector, 'shove a little back, more to the left, the sun bothers me, that will do—now young Master step this way. I will learn you to see and catch flat-fish —There,' pointing with his spear, 'don't you see those eyes, how they shine like diamonds.'—'very good now,' says he, I will strike it in the head,' and away went his iron and the clear bottom was nothing but a cloud of moving sand, caused by the death struggle—The fish proved to be a large flounder and the way old Hector shouted was a caution to all wind instruments. . . . "

25. LOSS AND GAIN

1847

Oil on canvas, 24 x 20 in.

MR. AND MRS. J. WILLIAM MIDDENDORF, II, NEW YORK

MC: "Year 1847 . . . Loss & Gain—painted for R.F. Fraser, Esq. Price one hundred and seventy-five dollars. On Canvas—size I believe 17 by 21."

Mount to George P. Morris, (Editor of the *New York Mirror*) *December 3, 1854:* "The manner in which you introduced my picture, 'Sportsman at the Well' in your art notices I am pleased with, also that you intend to give a description of it should it ever 'journey back from this place and find a nook' somewhere in the City. I hope it may be so fortunate as to find so good a resting place among so many interesting works of art.

"Allow me to detain you a moment and relate to you why I took the above picture home with me. I painted it with a view to have it owned by the Art-Union for distribution, as a number of my friends wished to see several of my pictures in that institution. Accordingly I invited one of the Committee, I believe a warm friend to see it. He saw it and advised me to send it to the office of the Art-Union, that the committee would not meet on Thursday evening the 2d of Nov. and that I should know in the morning the result. The next day I called at the Office and was told that the Committee concluded not to vote on so high priced a picture (only three hundred including frame) until a larger meeting which would take place in about twenty days. I thought it was a delicate hint that my picture was not wanted. I took it down from the walls of the Committee room and departed.

"I have never sold but two pictures to the Art Union and was beat down in my price on one of those. Last year they gave me an order, the only one I ever received from that quarter. I completed the picture in time, and it gave satisfaction. The one now in the Art-Union—'Loss and Gain'—was not obtained from me, I sold it to Robert F. Fraser, Esq. The Art Union does not give orders this year, but intend to buy pictures at low prices to grind the artist down. They suspect the arts are getting too high for Crockery Merchants & Tape Sellers. Therefore something must be done to make the art succumb, and it cannot be done more effectually than by rejecting pictures of the artists. I am convinced that such a system in the end will produce poor pictures, and the insulted public (that pay their personal subscription of membership, *five dollars*) will inquire why they and the artist are not better treated.

"I will add, the Committee rejected on the same evening a beautiful picture by S.A. Mount, a piece of still life (Shell fish, Price Fifty dollars). They left word with a tall, genteel looking Englishman engaged in the office—that the picture was too shelly. What impudence, when my brother had been requested by one of the Committee to paint a picture of the kind for them. I have been told that some of the Committee of the Art-Union are so noble in their views of art (in their efforts for the 'promotion of the Fine Arts') that they would gladly see pictures sold by the Yard measure. Artists will be compelled to exhibit and sell their own works as heretofore in their own rooms. Mr. Matteson and Mr. Stearns told me that they had already adopted that plan for their own safety and dignity as artists."

To the draft of this letter which he preserved, Mount added a passage with the notation that it was not included in the copy sent to Morris:

"A few days since, a stranger asked me how much money it required to become a member of the National Academy of Design. He thought the Art Union and the National Academy were all one thing.

"Let every artist ask himself if he does not feel more pride in having his pictures exhibited in the National Academy. If he had not rather have his pictures rejected by a committee of Artists than by a committee of Merchants. Art Unions are a sign of art in distress and serves to lower the dignity of artists—and gives out this idea to the world that the artists as a body art not capable of self government. In the first place, who paints the pictures, the committee of the Art Union or the artists? I through out these ideas for reflection."

26. SHEPARD ALONZO MOUNT

1847

Oil on canvas, 24 x 28 in.

SUFFOLK MUSEUM AND CARRIAGE HOUSE, MELVILLE COLLECTION, STONY BROOK, LONG ISLAND

MC: "Head and bust of Shepard A. Mount, N.A., size 18 x 24, painted May 5, 1847."

In addition to William, three members of the Mount family engaged in the art of painting—his brothers, Henry and Shepard, and Henry's daughter, Evalina. Henry (1802-1841) got a late start, died relatively young, and accomplished relatively little. Evalina was a hopeless amateur. Shepard, however, was fully as professional an artist as William Sidney, and he confronts the student of William Sidney with serious problems.

Shepard was three years older than William but began his career at about the same time, after several years' apprenticeship to James Brewster, the coach maker in New Haven. Shepard and William were trained in the same school (the National Academy of Design), used the same techniques, and painted in and for the same class of people; it is therefore not surprising to find William stating in his diary, "Yesterday, August 11th 61 I assisted my brother in touching up some of his portraits." All this makes for considerable difficulty in establishing the differential diagnosis between the styles of the two artists.

Shepard seems to have painted less genre than William Sidney and to have been much less successful in this mode; his anecdote lacks the incisive, dramatic quality of William's, and his figure draughtsmanship in genre is less crisp. Shepard's portraits, like William's, are exceedingly uneven in quality, but a first-rate portrait by Shepard can hold its own in any company. Shepard traveled more extensively than William. His portraits are scattered all over the eastern seaboard; many are lost, and many, doubtless, have been attributed to other artists.

On October 5, 1837, Shepard married Elizabeth Elliott, sister of the celebrated portrait painter, Charles Loring Elliott. One result of this was to bring William Sidney close to his brother's brother-in-law; he wrote about him constantly, visited his studio, painted his portrait, adopted his methods, and delighted in everything he did. But Elizabeth caused estrangement between William and Shepard, as witness a diary entry of William's in 1852 or 1853:

"My sister-in-law, Mrs. S.A. Mount, has not thought proper to speak to me in one year, a long time, when she could be so agreeable. I believe she has regard & friendship for me, but her husband is opposed to her being friendly to me. I am sorry to say it. I wish them both well—yet the extraordinary manner in which they have acted toward me the last three years leads me to believe what I have stated."

This is the only hint of a sentimental relationship on William's part in all his diaries and letters. Elizabeth died in 1858, and after her death the brothers were reconciled. Shepard died on September 18, 1868, two months and one day before the sudden, unexpected death of William.

The only study of Shepard so far published is *Shepard Alonzo Mount*, the catalogue of an exhibition held at the Heckscher Art Museum in Huntington, Long Island, in 1945, with a biographical sketch by Albert D. Smith.

27. THE NOVICE

1847

Oil on canvas, 30 x 25 in.

SUFFOLK MUSEUM AND CARRIAGE HOUSE, MELVILLE COLLECTION, STONY BROOK, LONG ISLAND

MC: "Year 1847 . . . The Novice—painted expressly for the Art Union. I received three hundred the price agreed upon. Canvass 25 x 30."

Charles Lanman to Mount, September 7, 1847: "I have seen your picture of the Novice. I like it hugely, —the expression and drawing are faultless. In one or two particulars, friend Mount you have been a little careless. (Now don't frown upon me my friend, for you know I think you the greatest painter on the continent). How do you manage to throw the same tone of color alike over that brick wall, that stick of timber, the underpining and the ground? Is it right? I think too that the shadows of your whites are not *exactly* the thing, they are too yellowish: and there is not quite atmosphere enough in the landscape. You have triumphed in the two grand features of a picture, but in color you can do better. Forgive me my dear Mount and write to me soon."

Mount to Lanman, September 9, 1847: " . . . I am pleased you like my picture of the Novice and speak so free of it. I know in some particulars I could have improved it & desired to take it home for that purpose but Mr. Fraser and another Gent would not listen to it—said they were pleased with it as it was—that they were disappointed in obtaining a picture from me—did not believe I would have a picture in time—it was good enough, and so on. For my part I wish it was better though I labored honestly for the Art Union. In many respects I think it my best picture. However it will be well to leave that for others to say. Mr. Patterson, a friend of mine and a lover of painting, says that it is the most brilliant in colour that I have painted. So thinks George W. Austin.

"In the Novice I wished to preserve breadth and to tell my story. If figures are the principal, everything else should be subordinate, depending on the taste of the artist. When landscape is primo, and figures are introduced, they are and must be secondo. See Coles and Durands landscapes in the Art Union or look at Claude's landscapes. On the contrary, look at Murillos productions, all is sacrificed for the good of the figures. But what is the use of my talking in this way when you understand so well the principles of the art.

"As regards the Art Union, the plan of giving orders and having the gallery free to the public is a good one, and highly approved of by the number of subscribers. I should have been pleased to have painted for the committee years ago, had they given me orders, but they could not expect me to paint upon uncertainty, when I had orders from private individuals to execute. Finally, the managers of the Art Union appear to be on the right road, and we must give them three cheers for what they have done and what they expect to do . . . "

28. FARMER WHETTING HIS SCYTHE

1848

Oil on canvas, 20 x 24 in.

SUFFOLK MUSEUM AND CARRIAGE HOUSE, MELVILLE COLLECTION, STONY BROOK, LONG ISLAND

MC: "Year 1847 . . . A Farmer whetting his scythe. On canvass, 20 x 24. I gave it to the" [*stricken out and illegible*] "it was bought with others for the Art Union."

Whitney Journal, December 9, 1848: "I finished this day a picture Long Island Farmer whetting his scythe. By toning over the sky and distance, with blue, red, and yellow, in this instance I let the Lake predominate—giving a beautiful aerial warmth."

Whitney Journal, Page 124: " . . . Farmer whetting his sythe—painted on the spot."

31. CALIFORNIA NEWS

1850

Oil on canvas, 21⅛ x 20¼ in.

SUFFOLK MUSEUM AND CARRIAGE HOUSE, MELVILLE COLLECTION, STONY BROOK, LONG ISLAND

MC: "Year 1850, California News or Reading the Tribune painted on canvass—Size 18 in by 20 in for Thos McElrath Esqr. Price $300.00."

Whitney Journal, December 22, 1848: "For about two months past there has been great excitement about the Gold Placers in North California. Thousands are rushing there to have a hand in sifting & picking— I hope it may turn out a blessing to the country—than a curse. We should be thankful for the gold that we get directly from the hands of the Almighty—and make good use of it."

Thomas McElrath was one of the publishers of the *New York Daily Tribune;* hence the importance given that newspaper in this painting. The man in the slouch hat at the right of the table is Mount himself and the children and young adults are traditionally said to be his niece and nephews. The picture of pigs above the door is copied from a painting by William Sidney's brother, Henry Smith Mount. For Mount to put himself and his family so prominently into a genre picture is highly unusual and suggests that the painting may originally have had some covert meaning now lost.

29. JUST IN TUNE

1849

Oil on canvas, 30 x 25 in.

SUFFOLK MUSEUM AND CARRIAGE HOUSE, MELVILLE COLLECTION, STONY BROOK, LONG ISLAND

MC: "First of Nov.—1849—I sold a picture—Just in tune, To George J. Price Esqr—painted on canvass 25 x 30. price including frame one hundred & fifty dollars—It is to be engraved in Paris by Emile La-salle."

Oscar Bullis to Mount, September 24, 1849: "...I do wish you would allow the public to see your 'California Boy'—that mischievous looking dog tuning his violin preparatory to a 'breakdown'—If you will let me have it, I will be answerable for its safety and I will procure its exhibition in one of the parlours of the Astor and will engage that a number of southerners that are now on here shall see it—I do really think you can find a purchaser for it on your own terms—If I could afford to buy that picture I would give you $1000 for it without winking..."

Just in Tune is mentioned in the anonymous article about William Schaus and his interest in Mount an extract from which appears in our notes on *Catching Rabbits*. It is one of four studies by Mount of single figures with musical instruments which Schaus caused to have reproduced in Paris and published by Goupil, Vibert, and Company. The other three are *Right and Left*, *The Banjo Player*, and *The Bones Player*, all of which are in the present exhibition.

30. RAFFLING FOR A GOOSE, after THE LUCKY THROW

Lithograph after Mount, by Jean-Baptiste Adolphe Lafosse. 25 x 19⅝. Published by Goupil and Company, Paris, London, Berlin, New York, 1851.

This work was conceived by William Schaus, Goupil's New York agent, as a companion piece to *Just in Tune*. Mount also painted *Right and Left*, *The Banjo Player*, and *The Bones Player* for reproduction under Schaus's auspices, and the five pictures form a kind of cycle or series. *The Lucky Throw*, however, is the only one of the five that does not involve musical instruments. The original canvas is lost; we therefore represent it with the lithograph, and, at the same time, exemplify the type of print which played so important a role in Mount's career.

Schaus occasionally changed the titles of Mount's paintings when he made prints of them, apparently in an effort to establish a distinction between the original and the reproduction. He was very inconsistent about this, however, and in selecting *Raffling for a Goose* as the alternative title for the present lithograph he caused confusion with the entirely different Mount painting of that name produced in 1837; this painting is also in the present show.

Whitney Journal, September 15, 1850: Pictures for Wm Schaus, Esqr.

"One picture (life size head) 25 x 30. An old man of the Revolutionary times reading an account of the battle of Bunker Hill—Paper and costumes of the times.

"One picture—Negro—African—head life size—Laughing and showing his white teeth and holding something funny in his hand—Goose, a Duck, or a squirrel &c. 25 x 30.

"One picture cabinet size—Negro asleep in a barn while a little boy is tickling his foot. Another a group of figures, Reading the Herald.

"A group of figures Talking—seated around in a circle.

"Courtship. A Negro popping the question. Only think of that.

"Bone player. Banjo player."

MC: "I have just completed a picture of a Negro—the lucky throw—on canvass, 25 x 30. Painted Dec. 1850."

47

32. RIGHT AND LEFT

1850

Oil on canvas, 30 x 25 in.

SUFFOLK MUSEUM AND CARRIAGE HOUSE, MELVILLE COLLECTION, STONY BROOK, LONG ISLAND

MC: "Year 1850 . . . One picture for the house of Goupil & Co. A Negro, 'Right and Left' on canvass 25 x 30 price $150.00. To be engraved in Paris."

See our notes on *Catching Rabbits* and *Just in Tune.*

Note that the hero of this painting bows with his left hand and fingers the violin with his right; hence the title. When the picture was lithographed in Paris, it was copied directly onto the stone; consequently in the print he plays like a proper violinist.

33. WHO'LL TURN THE GRINDSTONE? (illustration on page 50)

1851

Oil on canvas, 25 x 30 in.

SUFFOLK MUSEUM AND CARRIAGE HOUSE, MELVILLE COLLECTION, STONY BROOK, LONG ISLAND

MC: "Year 1851. One picture, "Who'll turn Grindstone.' Painted for Jonathan Sturges Esqr. on canvas size 29 x 36. Price $300.00."

Mount often assembled long lists of ideas for pictures under the general heading "Subjects." In December, 1844, he jotted down the following under that designation:

"Two lovers walking out. Walking out after marriage, one after the other — after the manner of Jude and Sam. The husband two months after marriage, with a bag of grain on his shoulder going to mill. A Whig after the Election. A Clergyman looking for a sermon at the bottom of his barrel. A Negro fiddleing on the crossroads on Sunday. Kite broke loose. Claming and fishing. Farmer feeding hogs — office holder. Croton Water. Land Mark, or strengthen the Memmory. Creeping for a wood chuck. Please to give me a penny. Cold victuals. Blowing rocks. A Group listening to the Grand spy. Have you an ax to grind." (*Footnote to this last:* "Who'll turn grindstone.") "The Tribune in the country. Curtain lecture. A poor widow about to part with relics of better days in order to supply bread for her starving children. Entertaining a clergyman. Boys listening to an old vetran fifer. A short history of Mr. Dignity. Camp meeting. Last of the Montauks. A poor Artist sketching his foot while his wife is busy washing his shirt."

When Mount actually painted one of the subjects in these lists, he would score it through lightly to indicate that fact. The only subjects so treated here are "Who'll turn grindstone" and "The Tribune in the Country," which was ultimately realized as *The Herald in the Country.*

Mount to Jonathan Sturges*, March 14, 1851: "I thank you for waiting so patiently for your picture. It is almost finished. I shall endeavor to make it creditable to both of us, so that we shall be able to go down to posterity clinging to the skirts of Dr. Franklin's coat tail — I believe he is the *author* of 'Who'll turn Grindstone.' It has engaged my attention from time to time ever since you gave me the commission.

"I expect to be in the City about the 20th inst. with the picture. I hope Mr. Conely will have the frame ready."

Sturges to Mount, March 17, 1851: "Your esteemed favor of the 14th inst. is recd, announcing the fact

*For Sturges, see our notes on *Farmers Nooning.*

that there is a prospect that you and I are likely to have a chance to go down to posterity clinging to Dr. Franklin's skirts.

"For that purpose, and at the same time to get hold of your 'coat tail' in case the other should not be sufficient, I shall be most happy to take a 'turn at your grindstone'

"The fact is, I have been waiting so long to get a 'turn' that I can hardly wait for you to get here with it. I have no doubt it will be of the *real grit* (?) such as usually comes from *your quarry.*

"Had Sketch Club last Friday evening, grand time, wish you had been there. we miss you from amongst us and wish you were within hailing distance."

When *Who'll Turn the Grindstone* was exhibited at the National Academy of Design in 1851, the catalogue contained an anecdote credited to the *Essays of Poor Robert the Scribe*, a title for which one will search in vain among the writings of Benjamin Franklin:*

"'I am sure that you are one of the finest lads I have ever seen, will you just turn a few minutes for me?' Tickled with the flattery, like a little fool, I went to work, and bitterly did I rue the day. It was a new axe, and I toiled and tugged, till I was almost tired to death. The school bell rung, and I could not get away; my hands were blistered and it was not half ground. At length, however, the axe was sharpened, and the man turned to me, with 'Now you little rascal, you've played the truant—scud to school or you'll rue it.' Alas, thought I, it was hard enough to turn grindstone this cold day, but now to be called 'little rascal' was too much. It sunk deep into my mind and often have I thought of it since."

This painting is unique among the genre pictures of Mount in requiring that the spectator be familiar with a prose anecdote in order to understand its story. In every other instance, Mount's painted anecdote is perfectly clear and self-sufficient and does not even require a title to be entirely intelligible.

Essays from the Desk of Poor Robert the Scribe is one of the pseudo-Franklinian collections which were the stock in trade of numerous American writers during the early years of the nineteenth century. These essays were written by a Pennsylvania journalist named Charles Miner and were published in book form in 1815.

34. THE HERALD IN THE COUNTRY

1853

Oil on panel, 17 x 13 in.

SUFFOLK MUSEUM AND CARRIAGE HOUSE, MELVILLE COLLECTION, STONY BROOK, LONG ISLAND

MC: "Year 1853 . . . Politics of 1852, or Who let down the bars, panel, 13 x 17 in. Sold to Goupil & Co. $150.00."

Goupil and Company to Mount, March 21, 1854: "The painting 'laying down the bars' is coming back and the lithograph completed. Our house in Paris requests us to send them a good title for the print. Last time we saw you, you spoke of another than the above said one, if you think one would be better, please inform us at your convenience and oblige."

The title, *The Herald in the Country*, is given on Goupil's lithograph, which was published simultaneously in New York, London, Paris, and Berlin. Goupil obviously thought that Mount's original title was too parochial in its implications for an international audience; hence the request for a change.

The phrase, *Politics of 1852*, or *Who Let Down the Bars?*, would seem to imply some hidden political meaning, but this does not seem to be Mount's intention. Franklin Pierce, the Democratic candidate for President, was elected by a landslide in 1852, and Mount was a faithful Democrat; furthermore, the Compromise of 1850 was reaffirmed by Pierce's election, and no bars were let down. The point of the picture seems merely to be that the dandified hunter (who bears a far from accidental resemblance to Mount himself) has been caught by the countryman poaching on his land and has pulled the newspaper from his pocket and started to talk about the campaign in order to distract the countryman's attention from the dead game bird at the lower left.

35. WALKING OUT

1854

Oil on canvas, 27 x 22 in.

SUFFOLK MUSEUM AND CARRIAGE HOUSE, MELVILLE COLLECTION, STONY BROOK, LONG ISLAND

Not listed in MC.

George Searing to Mount, January 27, 1855 (from New Orleans): "I herewith hand Judson & Co. on G.S. Robbins & Son, sight, Fifty Dollars, being an installment on 'Walking Out.'

"I regret I cannot report much improvement in Mrs. Searing's health, she is better than she was last winter but not so well as this [illegible] summer. We intend making a trip to Ocean Springs (on Lake Ponchartrain) hopeing the mineral waters, change of air, etc. may prove beneficial.

"We should be pleased to hear from you with a little history of what has transpired in the village during our absence."

Searing is an old Long Island name, and there is a Searingtown not far from Stony Brook.

According to Cowdrey and Williams, *Walking Out* is a group portrait of Mrs. George Searing and her two daughters. The work is a good example of the mingling of genre and portraiture which is characteristic of much nineteenth century American painting.

36. THE BANJO PLAYER

c.1855

Oil on canvas, 25 x 30 in.

THE DETROIT INSTITUTE OF ARTS

On August 19, 1874, Mount's heirs, Robert and Thomas Mount and Ruth H. Seabury, submitted to the Surrogate's Court for Suffolk County, New York, an accounting of their administration of William Sidney's estate. It contains the following statement:

"The settlement of the estate has been one of unusual difficulty. The deceased was unmarried. He died after a very sudden illness of a few days duration. The extent of his property, its location, and the nature of it, except the articles apparent to everyone, were unknown. His effects were much scattered. It was not until after a protracted and diligent search that any evidence of deposit was discovered. Considerable personal property consisted of oil paintings. A few were finished, the most unfinished, and some barely commenced. . . .

"In April, 1871, about thirty-three pictures and sketches were offered for sale at public auction by Robert Somerville at his salesroom in Fifth Avenue in the city of New York. The result of such sale is hereto annexed."

Somerville's attached list mentions a *Banjo Player*, offered at fifty dollars, but left unsold. This, in all probability, is the Detroit picture. Charles J. Werner told Cowdrey and Williams that *The Banjo Player in the Barn* was unfinished, and that Mount intended to add other figures dancing in the background. This would account for the absence of the picture from MC and Mount's correspondence, the low price asked for it at Somerville's sale, and the fact that it had no takers. We may be thankful, however, that Mount did not complete *The Banjo Player in the Barn*, for the empty space, the lonely figure, and the dark tonality of the painting produce an Eakins-like somberness which is unique in Mount's work.

37. THE BANJO PLAYER

1856

Oil on canvas, 36 x 29 in.

SUFFOLK MUSEUM AND CARRIAGE HOUSE, MELVILLE COLLECTION, STONY BROOK, LONG ISLAND

38. THE BONES PLAYER

1856

Oil on canvas, 36 x 29 in.

MUSEUM OF FINE ARTS, BOSTON, M. & M. KAROLIK COLLECTION

MC: "Year 1856 . . . Bone Player—a Negro—painted on canvass 29 x 36. for Wm Schaus Esqr for publication. Sold to John D. Jones Esqr $200.00 Mr. Schaus paid me one hundred—100.00—for the copy right. finished April 3d — Banjo Player, a Negro, companion to the above, painted on canvass 29 x 36, for Mr. Schaus for publication. Sold to Charles M. Leupp Esq. for $200.00. Sold the copy right to Mr. Schaus—100.0 The above pictures are now being engraved in Paris. When the Banjo player returns Mr Leupp will pay me. Oct. 1857, have received pay."

William Schaus to Mount, September 1, 1852: " . . . You know how anxious I am to publish more of your works as soon as possible and I should be pleased to know if I could obtain the following pictures:

"'Raffling for a goose' (now in Troy I believe)

"Negro asleep—'Hay Making'

"'Bargaining for a horse.

"I do not wish to obtain the copyrights *gratis, but I intend allowing you an interest on the sale of each copy.* As long as I was Agent for Messrs. Goupil & Co. I was obliged to act in accordance to their instructions, but now I can be liberal on my own account and nobody can find fault with it. I would also give you an order for some large heads same size about of 'Just in Tune,' 'Right and Left,' and 'Raffling,' the subjects to be something like the above and [*illegible*]:

"'Negro playing the banjo and singing'

"'Negro playing with bones'

"How soon can I have one or both of these pictures? It is my wish that you shall derive an interest from the sale of all Engravings I may publish after your works. I should be pleased to see you previous to my departure. Please to consider this letter strictly confidential."

Mount to Schaus, September 9, 1852: "Your letter of September 1 I have received. I like the tone of it. The good feeling manifested. I am ready to negociate with you, if you will state the time when and where I can meet with you. I will undertake those large heads for you—although I have been urged not to paint any more such subjects. I had as leave paint the character of some negros as to paint the characters of some *whites* as far as the morality is concerned. 'A Negro is as good as a white man as long as he behaves himself.'"

Continued on page 56

Mount to Schaus, March 8, 1854: " . . . The pictures you desire me to paint are not commenced. I have not been well enough. To paint understandingly the mind must be clear. Health is important. Time will bring out the Negros and make them to shine like a full moon."

Mount to Schaus, March 26, 1856: "It affords me great pleasure to state that I am engaged painting The *Bone Player* for you—for publication—The size is 29½ in by 36½ inches—I will not say any thing about the painting, as your own eye will tell you better than a description from me—I expect to have the picture finished next week—You may prepair a *head* (round moulding) frame, to exhibit it in if you think proper, in your own store."

Whitney Journal, April 3, 1856: "I finished the bone player this day—over white ground. I rubbed the canvas over with venetian red—ground in oil thinned with turpentine—it should be used with drying oil—any color can be given in the above way—when dry commence painting—

"If the flesh of the negro should be too warm, when dry rub over thinly some blue—to cool it down— I painted the above picture without varnish—Boild oil and raw oil—The latter drys fast enough in hot weather—It is thought to be more durable—more limped your colors the better you work.

"April 6, 1856—

"I expect to take my Bone Player to the City tomorrow. When I return I shall take board down in the village for the sake of exercise and change. Some people incline to get saucy if you board with them too long—Particularly a young Lady that's been brought up in a boarding school."

Mount to E.L. Magoon, April 6, 1856: " . . . I have just finished a picture—The *Bone Player*, a Negro. The order was given two years ago—I had not the humor to paint it until lately . . . "

Whitney Journal, Page 165: "1856. Copy of a note from Mr. Schaus. My dear Sir, My commission to paint me a picture similar to 'Raffling for a Goose'* is to be in the following terms. Each picture to be $200—including the copy right. With a view to afford to you additional advantages, you are at liberty to sell the picture to any party and reserve me the copy right, and in that case I will give you one hundred dollars $100.00 for the copy right of each picture." *Note added by Mount:* "I have painted and sold two pictures (the bone and Banjo performers) according to the terms mentioned above—& receiving $100 copy right of each painting to be engraved."

Diary, May 24, 1858: "I painted the Banjo player in eight days (16 sittings) two sittings a day, the Bone player in seven days (or 14 sittings) two sittings a day forenoon and afternoon."

*As is pointed out elsewhere in these notes, the painting Schaus called *Raffling for a Goose* is not the Stony Brook tavern scene which belongs to the Metropolitan; it was a large Negro head like *The Bones Player* and *The Banjo Player.* The original of this painting is lost and it is known today only through Schaus's print of it. A copy of the print is in the present exhibition.

39. MARY FORD RICE

c.1860

Oil on panel, 18 x 14 in.

SUFFOLK MUSEUM AND CARRIAGE HOUSE, MELVILLE COLLECTION, STONY BROOK, LONG ISLAND

Mary Ford Rice (1858-1888) was the granddaughter of Mount's brother, Henry. She married the Reverend Dr. John Q. Archdeacon, and her son, Charles Q. Archdeacon, was one of the major collectors of Mountiana in the early years of the present century.

40. RETURNING FROM THE ORCHARD

1862

Oil on panel, 19¾ x 26¼ in.

SUFFOLK MUSEUM AND CARRIAGE HOUSE, MELVILLE COLLECTION, STONY BROOK, LONG ISLAND

MC: "March 31st 1862. I have just finished two pictures (they were commenced in my Stony Brook studio) Returning from the Orchard size 19¾ x 26¼ on wood—Going Trapping on canvass—25 x 30. The above not sold—(Sold 1864, $325.00.)"

Mount to H.W. Derby, June 30, 1862: "You ask if the paintings are for sale, prices—'Returning from the Orchard' with frame, two hundred and seventy-five dollars. 'Going Trapping' three hundred dollars without frame . . . I value this at $350. The two at $300. But owing to the times I will sell at the above named prices and retain the copy right. These are the only pictures I have for sale at present."

But Mount did not sell *Returning from the Orchard*. It is listed among the pictures found in his studio after his death and offered for sale by Robert Somerville of New York in 1871, at a price of $180, without takers.

41. CATCHING CRABS

1865

Oil on canvas, 18 x 24 in.

SUFFOLK MUSEUM AND CARRIAGE HOUSE, MELVILLE COLLECTION, STONY BROOK, LONG ISLAND

Diary, March 19, 1865: "Glazed over the lower part of the 'Catching crabs' with madder lake and raw sienna—warm oil (bleached) & damar together, added a little boiled oil—glazed the sky with madder lake alone, rubbed all in with the palm of my hand . . ."

Diary, July 5, 1865: "Sold two more paintings to Chas B. Wood Esqr. four works that were on exhibition at the N. Academy—They were:

"*Peace*—size 22 x 27 on canvass—

"Catching Crabs canvas 18 x 24—

"Loitering by the way, on panel—size 14 x 19¾

"Early impressions are lasting panel size 11⅞ x 9¾.

"Mr. Wood paid for the paintings:

"Peace	$300.00
"Early impressions	$150.00
"Loitering	$200.00
"Catching Crabs	$250.00
	$900.00"

Charles B. Wood was one of Mount's most enthusiastic supporters during his last years. According to a diary entry of May 24, 1858, Wood had recently offered to set Mount up in a New York studio and buy every other painting he produced. Shortly after, in a list of possible subjects, one reads "'Jairus Daughter' for Mr. Wood," as if to imply that Mount intended to paint a new version of that old subject for this patron; this is backed up by another diary jotting of 1858 wherein Mount records that Wood has ordered two pictures from him, one to be a scriptural subject. In the spring of 1859, Mount spent ten weeks as Wood's house guest at 36 Laight Street, New York, and Wood at that time offered to subsidize the artist for the summer so that he would be free to study landscape from nature. In October of 1859, Wood invited Mount to New York to paint his portrait; in December Mount reiterates that Wood wants a Biblical painting by him.

Concerning his ten weeks in Woods's house, Mount made the following remarks in his catalogue of paintings:

"For the time I spent at Mr. Woods, touching up some of his paintings (during the months of February and March) I charged nothing, but I was well treated. In some respects it was a benefit, but I do not wish to try the experiment again. New York City is the place to make an artist work—he is stimulated by the works of others—Fortunate for me, two Exhibitions of French and English paintings were open to the public. I spent two or three weeks studying them. It is well enough to look at the works of others but not to copy; to observe design, drawing, and how colors are contrasted."

On June 1, 1862, Mount offered Wood his painting, *Going Trapping*, for three hundred dollars, fifty dollars less than the established price for that work. Wood declined twenty days later because he had "resolved not to speculate in Pictures of my artist friends;" nevertheless he did buy the picture, on May 7, 1864, for $325; "it was worth much more," says Mount in his diary-entry recording that transaction.

On June 6, 1864, Wood wrote Mount one of the most curious letters in his entire correspondence:

"I purchased at the 'Waldo sale' some of those pannels, nine of them 26 x 33, three 28 x 36; three 24 x 30; two, 22 x 27. Most of them have the portraits of somebody's Grandfather or something on them—they cost but 75 cents each about what the wood is worth by the foot, if they are of any use to you you are quite welcome to them . . . In framing your 'Boys Going Trapping' I thought of making it of carved wood with something appropriate in the design to the subject similar to the accompanying sketch. The animals are supposed to be rabbits . . ." (The sketch is for a vertical frame with rabbits in various positions and with a box trap like the one in Mount's *Deadfall* of 1844 in the lower left corner.)

Mount replied on June 9, accepting the panels, stating that he would have them planed off, and giving instructions for their shipment to Setauket. As regards Wood's sketch for a frame, Mount suggests substituting "Apples & Grapes in place of box trap as it will be repeating the traps in the picture, or you can introduce a quail or partrages—or a woodchuck, skunk, or fox somewhere about the frame— as they have seen and felt a trap—have the heads without the bodies as you have marked out or a young rabbit running as you have marked out."

It is difficult to believe that after the death of the distinguished portrait painter, Samuel Lovett Waldo, in 1861, the panels in his studio were sold like so much raw lumber, but this seems to be the implication of Wood's letter.

42. FAIR EXCHANGE NO ROBBERY

1865

Oil on panel, 26 x 33 ½ in.

SUFFOLK MUSEUM AND CARRIAGE HOUSE, MELVILLE COLLECTION, STONY BROOK, LONG ISLAND

Diary, October 24, 1865: "Worked on the scare crow in the afternoon—it happened to be calm. Oct. of 65 has been *very boisterious.*"

Diary, November 15-16, 1865: "Painted on the scare crow or Robbing a cast off scare crow of a hat. 'Even exchange no robbery.'"

This painting was one of those offered for sale by Robert Somerville in 1871, at a price of $270. It was the most expensive picture at the Somerville sale, but it was not sold.

43. CATCHING THE TUNE

1866

Oil on canvas, 22 x 27 in.

SUFFOLK MUSEUM AND CARRIAGE HOUSE, MELVILLE COLLECTION, STONY BROOK, LONG ISLAND

Robert Nelson Mount to William Sidney, July 28, 1840: " . . . I saw recently a scene which I think will make a good picture. It was two musical characters. One was whistling a tune and the other was sitting in a listening attitude with violin in hand, ready to commence playing when his 'croney' had finished. The subject no doubt is a hacknied one, but I do not believe anyone has handled it as you can."

(Observe that this letter was written more than a quarter of a century before Mount acted on the suggestion it contained.)

Diary, July 10, 1866: "Commenced a picture on canvass 22 x 27. Catching a tune. *Possum Up a Gum Tree.* Three figures."

Diary, September 28, 1866: "Painted on 'Catching a tune.'"

Mount's interest in the violin was second only to his interest in painting. As far back as 1837 he had invented a new type of violin; he patented it in 1852, took space at industrial fairs to exhibit it, sought endorsements for it from eminent musicians, and was constantly tinkering with its form, its varnish, and its size. Mount's principal innovation lay in giving his violin a hollow back; this, he was convinced, would increase the power of its tone. In 1857 he eliminated the corners and constructed a violin with the narrow waist and peculiar F holes that appear in the instrument depicted in this painting.

Interestingly enough, Mount refers to the type of violin represented in *Catching the Tune* in a diary entry of April 17, 1866, not long before he began work on the picture:

"I forgot to mention that on Tuesday evening April 17, 1866, Mr. Henri Appi played on my hollow back violin at the sujestion of Mr. Harvy Dodsworth, the leader, and the latter invited me to take seat in the orchestra at Niblo's Theatre. Mr. Appi observed to me that the violin was powerful & a good orchestra instrument. It is the first made of this style of F holes [sketch] and narrow at the waist, thus: [sketch] Made in 1857." (The two sketches, one of the F holes and the other of the all-over appearance of the violin, are identical with the instrument to be seen in *Catching the Tune.*)

44. MARIA WINTHROP SEABURY

c.1867

Oil on canvas, 20½ x 17 ⅜ in.

SUFFOLK MUSEUM AND CARRIAGE HOUSE, MELVILLE COLLECTION, STONY BROOK,
LONG ISLAND

One of three known portraits by William Sidney Mount of a favorite niece, daughter of the artist's
sister, Ruth Mount Seabury.

45. LANDSCAPE

Undated

Oil on canvas, 41 x 50½ in.

THE BERKSHIRE MUSEUM, PITTSFIELD, MASSACHUSETTS, GIFT OF MR. ZENAS CRANE, 1915

This is the great mystery-piece of Mount's *oeuvre*. It has been continuously on exhibition at the Berkshire Museum since 1915, when it was presented to that institution by its founder, Zenas Crane. It is
one of the largest paintings Mount ever produced, and for this reason alone one would have thought
it might attract some attention, but there does not seem to be one word about it in print, nor can it
be verified through any sketch, diary entry, or comment in any letter of Mount's. It is not mentioned
by Cowdrey and Williams, in their Mount study of 1944—and these authors did not hesitate to call a
painting unauthentic if they thought it was. The style of the work is clearly that of Mount's last years.

Man with Flute

Mr. Kean as Coriolanus

Profile of a Boy

Sketch for "Raffling for a Goose"

Maria Weeks Underhill

Elizabeth Julia Underhill

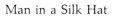

Man in a Silk Hat

Drawing from Hogarth's Works

upper left: Reading the News

left: Discussing the News

lower left: The Scarecrow

bottom left: The Mount House Kitchen

below: Sketch for "Power of Music" and
Sketch for "Dance of the Haymakers"

above: Mount's brother Robert

right: Two Theatre Sketches

LIST OF DRAWINGS BY WILLIAM SIDNEY MOUNT

MAN WITH FLUTE. 7 x 3-3/8 in.

MR. KEAN AS CORIOLANUS. 5-1/2 x 3-15/16 in.

PROFILE OF A BOY. 7 x 4-3/4 in.

SKETCH FOR "RAFFLING FOR A GOOSE". 7 x 4-7/16 in.

MARIA WEEKS UNDERHILL. 8-5/16 x 6-1/16 in.

ELIZABETH JULIA UNDERHILL. 8-1/4 x 6-1/4 in.

MAN IN A SILK HAT. 8-1/4 x 6-5/8 in.

DRAWING FROM HOGARTH'S WORKS. 9-3/4 x 8-3/4 in.

READING THE NEWS. 4-1/8 x 6-1/2 in.

DISCUSSING THE NEWS. 3-1/2 x 5-1/2 in.

THE SCARECROW. 3-1/2 x 5-1/4 in.

THE MOUNT HOUSE KITCHEN. 4-1/2 x 5-3/4 in.

SKETCH FOR "POWER OF MUSIC" AND
SKETCH FOR "DANCE OF THE HAYMAKERS". 8-7/8 x 5-1/2 in.

MOUNT'S BROTHER ROBERT. 3-5/8 x 3-1/8 in.

THEATRE SKETCH. 4-3/4 x 3-11/16 in.

THEATRE SKETCH. 4-5/8 x 3-11/16 in.

All drawings are lent by the Suffolk Museum at Stony Brook, Long Island.